C000262989

PRAISE FOR G

"*Gay is a GIFT* is Chicken Soup for the Gay Soul.
A+"   - *Web Digest Weekly*

"Salvatore Sapienza's *Gay is a GIFT* is itself a gift;
a sweet, inspiring portrayal of gay consciousness
as blessing, along with a simple, light-hearted -
even fun - spiritual practice for bringing more
blessing into your Life."
                    -Toby Johnson, *author of Gay Spirituality*

"**4 out of 4 stars**. A sweet epistle on gay
spirituality including some practical exercises as
well as personal anecdotes from the author's
personal struggle, it's a loving, worthwhile read."
                              -*Out Front Colorado*

"A fine offering of affirmation, information and
motivation that will raise both your spirits and
your consciousness. Sapienza's book illuminates
one man's struggle to eliminate the negativity of
being gay and replace it with the fine, white light
of positivism."   -*Out in Print*

"Use *Gay is a GIFT* as a guide and you will find yourself more at peace not just with yourself but with everyone. It is written so beautifully and says so much that, if you are like me, may find yourself reading it with tears in your eyes."

-Eureka Pride

PRAISE FOR *SEVENTY TIMES SEVEN*

"Required reading for gay persons of faith."
- *Q Media*

"A heartwarming read that will make a difference in your life."
-Gay Chicago Magazine

"Left me spellbound. Truly inspirational."
-PrideSource

"Urges readers to lead an honest, full life."
-GayWired

"Deeply moving and reverent."   *-EDGE Magazine*

"Recommended Reading" - Dan Savage, *Savage Love*

NOMINATED FOR 2 LAMBDA LITERARY
AWARDS INCLUDING BEST SPIRITUALITY

2

MYCHAL'S PRAYER

BY SALVATORE SAPIENZA
ILLUSTRATIONS BY DONNA LEONARD

Tregatti Press

Tregatti Press

Published by Tregatti Press
www.mychalsprayer.com

Published in the United States of America
Author Photo: Wyatt Lane
Mychal Judge Photo: AP

Mychal's Prayer/Salvatore Sapienza

ISBN: 978-0615473314

1.   Self-help   2. Body Mind Spirit
I. Title
Mychal's Prayer

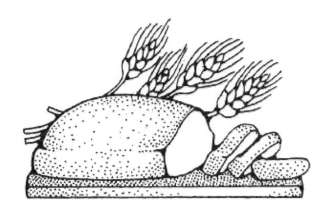

DEDICATED TO:

FATHER MYCHAL JUDGE, O.F.M.
(MAY 11, 1933 - SEPTEMBER 11, 2001)

"YOU HAVE NO IDEA
WHAT GOD IS CALLING YOU TO.
BUT HE NEEDS YOU. HE NEEDS ME.
HE NEEDS ALL OF US."

-FROM FATHER MYCHAL'S LAST HOMILY,
GIVEN ON SEPTEMBER 10, 2011

5

MYCHAL'S PRAYER:

LORD,
TAKE ME WHERE YOU WANT ME TO
GO

LET ME MEET WHO YOU WANT ME TO
MEET

TELL ME WHAT YOU WANT ME TO SAY

AND KEEP ME OUT OF YOUR WAY

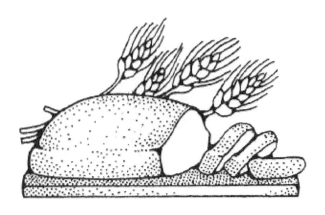

FOREWORD

Hagiography is a word given to the biography of a sainted person. These books are usually written in an overly pious manner, depicting the saints as super-holy individuals who are to be reverently worshipped on top of their pedestals. While these books are meant to inspire the devout, they can sometimes confound the sensibilities of the modern reader.

Reading about holy men and women with bleeding eyes or those who could levitate or bilocate at will may inspire awe, but they may also distance the reader, espousing an almost unattainable standard of spiritual enlightenment reserved only for a special few individuals.

Mychal's Prayer is not a hagiography, nor is it even a biography on the life of Father Mychal Judge, but rather a small devotional guidebook for integrating his personal prayer into your own life and your relationship with God.

This book is designed to be read in a meditative way, slowly and deliberately, in a prayerful manner. If a particular word or sentence speaks to you, stay with it, maybe underlining or highlighting it or writing it in a prayer journal, if you keep one. This is a book that is more meant to be prayed in parts, rather than absorbed wholly, so take your time with it. Remember, it is in the silence that we hear the voice of God, so create a sacred space for reading *Mychal's Prayer*, a place where you can truly "be still and know."

Father Mychal Judge was indeed a sainted individual, but he would not want to be put up on a pedestal. Rather, the way he lived his life provides a clear roadmap to holiness attainable by each and every one of us in our own lifetimes. Enact his prayer into your daily life, and you - yes, *you* - will walk the path of holiness, the way of the saints.

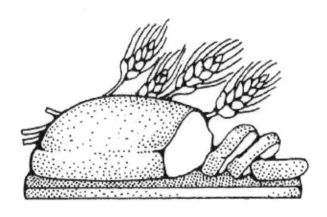

PREFACE

Though I have been praying Mychal's prayer for years now, I had not thought to write a book about it until I learned about Mama June.

Last year, I had the grace and blessing of receiving a letter from a reader letting me know that two of my previous books were the last ones he read aloud to his mother, June, before she finally succumbed to a long illness.

In those books, I recount the years of my life when I worked with Father Mychal Judge, and I also briefly mention the prayer Mychal prayed.

The letter writer, an openly gay man, let me know that his mother, a devout Catholic but also a proud PFLAG (Parents and Friends of Lesbians and Gays) mom, was so moved by Mychal's prayer that she requested it be on the prayer cards given at her funeral.

In the envelope along with the letter, the man sent me two of those prayer cards, one of which I will cherish and the other which I gave to my own mother.

A few months later, I recounted this story on a radio program in which I was being interviewed about my last book. Afterwards, I was contacted by several listeners who wanted me to send them the words to Mychal's prayer, as I had read them too quickly on the air.

During my morning meditation one day, I was expressing gratitude for these readers and listeners and, of course, for Mychal and his prayer, and that's when inspiration hit: There should be a book about Mychal's prayer.

Mychal had expressed several times that he wanted to write a book someday, but, sadly, he never got the opportunity. I hope that this book, *Mychal's Prayer*, published on the tenth anniversary of his transition, will help give voice to his legacy of love, service and surrender.

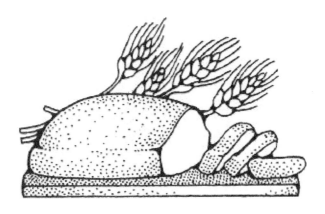

INTRODUCTION

On the morning of September 11, 2001, Father Mychal Judge, a Franciscan priest and chaplain of the New York City Fire Department, heard news of an explosion at the World Trade Center from a fellow friar in his community, and he immediately rushed to the site. As he offered aid and prayers to the fire fighters and the injured, Mychal was killed when the south tower collapsed.

A photograph of Mychal's body being carried out of the rubble by five uniformed men has since become one of the most famous images of 9/11. His body bag was labeled "Victim 0001," officially signifying Mychal as the first recorded victim of the attacks.

Though the world got to know him after that fateful day, Father Mychal and I became acquainted about fifteen years prior. At the time, I was in the Marist novitiate program in New York City studying to be a religious brother in the Catholic Church.

During the novitiate, we young brothers were encouraged to do some volunteer work in the community. As New York City was one of the places hardest hit by HIV at the time, I felt called to minister to people with AIDS.

Though I wanted to do something to help, most of the AIDS organizations in the city were very political with angry protest marches, many directed at the Catholic Church. One day, however, I noticed a small ad in the back of a weekly New York City gay news magazine announcing Saint Francis AIDS Ministry and seeking volunteers.

When I arrived at the Franciscan residence on 31st Street in Manhattan, I was met by Father Mychal, a larger-than-life figure with a warm smile and jovial personality. Over the next few weeks, Mychal mentored me and four other young men as we visited hospitals together and ministered to people with AIDS throughout the city.

Though grateful to serve, I was extremely anxious, telling Mychal that I was often unsure what to say to people as I approached their bedsides. He reassured me, telling me that God would give me the words to say, and if not, then I should just be quiet and present. It was great advice.

Watching Mychal minister to those in need was inspirational. He acted without fear and was entirely in the moment. The love and affection he showed was wholehearted and sincere. I learned a lot during my years working with Mychal, but, sadly, I did not keep in touch with him after I made the decision to leave religious life.

A decade later, after Mychal's death, I received a prayer card that was given out at his funeral.

On it was written: "*Mychal's Prayer: Lord, take me where you want me to go. Let me meet who you want me to meet. Tell me what you want me to say, and keep me out of your way.*" I openly wept as I read it, remembering the similar advice he gave me when I was a young man.

Since then, I have made this prayer a part of my daily life. It has brought me so much peace, so much joy, so much closer to God.

This book you're holding, *Mychal's Prayer*, is not really about me, though, or even about Father Mychal Judge, for that matter. Though you'll learn a little about both of us along the way, this book is really about you, and I trust you will learn mostly about yourself as you begin to incorporate Mychal's beautiful prayer into your daily life.

This is a book for people of all faiths and belief systems. Though Mychal was a Roman Catholic priest who had a great love for his Church, he was very inclusive, and his prayer has deep meaning for all who seek to grow in consciousness.

"There were no boundaries to Mychal's love. He was very inclusive," says a fellow friar, Father Patrick Fitzgerald. "There was not an ounce of racism, sexism or religious discrimination in his bones. Since his death, many people have come forward from the four corners of the globe saying that they had experienced Mychal's loving care and concern - poor people, rich people, Catholics and Muslims, men and women of all persuasions."

A great example of this inclusiveness was Mychal's ministry to the families of the people who were killed aboard the crash of a TWA Flight 800 off of Long Island, New York in 1996. Mychal drove back and forth between Manhattan and Queens every day for over two weeks, spending twelve hours a day at the Ramada Inn near J.F.K Airport consoling family members and friends who had lost loved ones. He consoled and counseled people of all religious denominations and celebrated an ecumenical memorial service which recognized the Oneness of all.

Another example of Mychal's inclusiveness was his ministry to the gay community, which often put him at odds with the Roman Catholic hierarchy in New York City.

Despite this, Mychal never backed down from his commitment to serve all of God's people, even those - *especially* those - who had been marginalized by the Church.

The library in Mychal's room was full of books from various faith traditions and from gay and lesbian authors. In keeping with this inclusiveness, this book shares the Universal Divine Wisdom shared by all the major world religions. You'll hear from Catholic saints, Hindu yogis, Buddhist monks, Jewish rabbis, New Thought scholars, and mystics, both old and new.

Of all the millions of books out in the world, this one somehow found its way to you. I believe there are no accidents or coincidences in our Divinely-ordered Universe, therefore I am confident that *Mychal's Prayer* is your prayer, too.

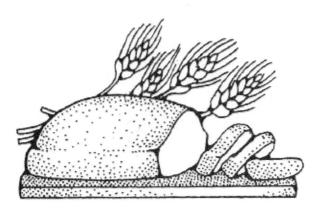

CHAPTER ONE

TAKE ME WHERE YOU WANT ME TO GO

THEME: *Surrender*

OPENING PRAYER:

*"Guide Thou my feet; compel my way; direct
my paths and keep me in Thy Presence."*
- Ernest Holmes, *Science of Mind*

ABOUT MYCHAEL:

A good friend once shared with me a
poem that he carries around in his wallet about
riding a tandem bike with God. It's about how in
the first half of your life, you are in the front seat
doing the steering, but, in the second half of your
life, when you learn surrender, you take the back
seat, unsure of the direction or the outcome, but
trusting in Spirit to lead you to pastures of
plenty.

In the second half of *his* life, Father Mychal Judge served as assistant to the president at Siena College in Loudonville, New York. The tall, handsome priest with the dazzling smile and bright blue eyes was a striking figure on campus, especially popular among the young student body for his down-to-Earth nature and sense of humor. One sign in his office read, "Here Come Da Judge," the line made famous at the time by TV comedian Flip Wilson and, of course, a play on Mychal's last name.

It was during this time, however, that Mychal became aware of a long-standing drinking problem. Though he showed no outward signs to those around him, Mychal realized there were times when he couldn't remember certain situations that happened to him when he was drinking socially. One morning, he awoke and discovered a shamrock tattoo on his rear end!

In 1978, Mychal attended his first Alcoholics Anonymous meeting, and he remained faithful to its assistance until the day he died, taking the eleventh step of the twelve-step program to heart.

Maybe this is where Mychal learned surrender, for Step 11 reads: *"Sought through prayer and meditation to improve our conscious contact with God as we understood Him, praying only for knowledge of His will for us and the power to carry that out."*

This is exactly how Mychal lived the rest of his life, not only in regards to alcohol, but also in his spiritual journey and priestly vocation. This is what he must have meant by the first line of his prayer, *"Lord, take me where you want me to go."* Mychal came to realize that true peace and joy could only come about through surrender.

Among the books on Mychal's bedroom shelves was an Alcoholic Anonymous guide for implementing the eleventh step. The guidelines contained in the book seem to apply to not only to Mychal's drinking, but to his entire state of being:

1. We ask God to direct our thinking, asking especially that it be divorced from self-pity, dishonest or self-seeking motives.

2. We consider our plans for the day. We can now use our mental faculties with assurance.

3. If we face indecision or we can't determine what course to take, we ask God for inspiration, an intuitive thought or a decision. We relax and take it easy.

4. We pray to be shown all through the day what our next step is to be, that we be given whatever we need to take care of problems.

5. We ask especially for freedom from self-will.

6. We ask for guidance in the way of patience, kindness, tolerance and love especially within the family.

7. We pray as to what we can do today for the person who is still sick.

8. If appropriate, we attend to our religious devotions, or say set prayers which emphasize 12 Step principles.

9. We may read from a spiritual book.

10. We pause, when agitated or doubtful, and ask for the right thought or action.

11. We constantly remind ourselves we are no longer running the show, humbly saying to ourselves many times each day "Thy will be done."

This theme of "Thy will be done" was overwhelmingly evident throughout the second half of Mychal Judge's life, as he surrendered himself completely to God's will in all of his endeavors. Like Mary, the mother of Jesus, to whom he had a great devotion, Mychal's answer to where God was taking him was always "yes."

Mary's "yes" to the Angel Gabriel's message from God, in which she states, "*I am the handmaid of the Lord. Let what you have said be done to me,*" was also Mychal's "yes." This "yes" was surely on Mychal's lips as he rushed to the World Trade Center on September 11, 2001.

There were reports from eyewitnesses at the scene that morning that Mychal was yelling, "*God, please end this right now!*" When I heard this, it reminded me of Jesus in Gethsemane, when he fell on his face and prayed, "*If it is possible, let his cup pass me by*" or later on the cross when he cried out, "*My God, my God, why have you deserted me?*"

As with Jesus' "*Nevertheless, let it be done to me as you, not I, would have it,*" Mychal, too, in his final moments was there to commit his spirit to the will of God and to give of his life so that others might live. This is "Thy will be done." This is sweet surrender.

Though I knew of Mychal's devotion to Mary, the thing I most often heard Mychal say was the Jesus Prayer, which reads, "Lord, Jesus Christ, Son of God, have mercy on me, a sinner." I had first become aware of this prayer in my first year of novitiate after reading a book by a 17th century monk named Brother Lawrence called *The Practice of the Presence of God*, where he talks about his use of the Jesus prayer, which he would recite throughout his day, whether he was peeling potatoes or washing pots and pans. It would, he said, realign his thoughts with God's.

Mychal would recite the Jesus Prayer throughout the day as we walked through hospital wards ministering to people with AIDS. Like with Brother Lawrence, I think it also brought Mychal "back to center."

Video footage of Mychal on September 11, 2001 standing outside the World Trade Center shows him visibly mumbling. Some witnesses present say he was praying to himself.

Though it's difficult to read his lips, I'd like to think he was reciting the Jesus Prayer, a prayer of surrender.

COMMENTARY:

Surrender seems like such a negative word, doesn't it? It's sounds like defeat, like giving up, like losing. And, in the world's terms, it is.

But, in the world of Spirit, surrender is not defeat, but freedom. This surrender is a "giving up of the egotistical, self-centered notion that I can direct and run my own life effectively and well…without conscious co-operation with the Spirit Within," so writes Thomas E. Powers in the book First *Questions on the Life of the Spirit.*

We see the importance of this in most faith systems and schools of thought. The word "Islam," for example, means "submission to God" and followers are called "Muslims," meaning "one who submits." The Bhagavad Gita, one of the most important Hindu scriptures, also urges its followers to "surrender your life to God."

Reverend Michael Bernard Beckwith, a best-selling spiritual writer and founder of the Agape Spiritual Center in Los Angeles, writes of the four-stages of spiritual growth and consciousness.

The first stage of consciousness is the "*TO ME*" stage. Much of the world is in this state of consciousness. It's the victim stage, in which we believe that everything is happening *TO* us. "*If only my spouse would be more loving...*" or "*If I had a better job, then I would...*" Life is happening *TO* you.

The second stage is "*BY ME*," which is when begin to understand that life is co-created by us and our thinking. When we learn to change our thoughts, we begin to change our circumstances, bringing about greater abundance and prosperity.

Though this is a wonderful discovery and state of consciousness, ultimately, Beckwith says, it's still about the world of form - about manifesting things like a new job or relationship or more money - so it will never truly satisfy us and it's not a place to stay.

The next stage - the third stage - is called "*THRU ME.*" This is the stage of surrender. It is here where we come to the understanding that we no longer need to direct. We are here to "let go" of our will and let Spirit work thru us. We begin to understand in this stage that we are a channel for grace, that life is happening thru us, and that's all that really matters, no matter our job or circumstance.

Finally, the forth stage is "*AS ME.*" These are the enlightened masters who understand and live moment by moment in the Christ Consciousness, Spirit AS ME, that Spirit and I are one in the same, as I believe Mychal ultimately did. This is the goal of the spiritual journey, but to get to this ultimate stage, we need to go thru and live Stage Three, which is surrender.

As with the eleventh step in Alcoholics Anonymous, this surrender is not a defeat, it's an awakening. Author Wayne Dyer says that "surrender is a sign of enlightenment and strength. It is not an abdication of responsibility, but rather the ultimate taking of responsibility. Surrender is a willingness to receive."

Like those seeking recovery, many of us are addicts: we are addicted to our negative thinking, our fears, thoughts of lack, of not being good enough, of our need to control.

Remember from the *Wizard of Oz* when Dorothy sees "Surrender, Dorothy" spelled in the sky? Well, think of those flying monkeys as the 'monkey mind' chatter that plays in our heads. This is the mind that is so focused on the past and the future; still holding on to the hurts of the past or worried about the future. Or the mind that wants to direct, making demands that God follow our schedule, rather than letting go and reminding ourselves that all is in Divine Order.

Jesus instructed Simon Peter to "feed my sheep" by telling him, "When you were young, you put on your own belt and walked where you liked; but when you grow old, you stretch out your hands, and somebody else will put a belt around you and take you where you would rather not go."

We need to surrender to the now present moment, to let go of those fears and worries and our need to direct. This is where Spirit lives, and it's here in the now present moment where we find peace. This is our true nature, peacefulness. Thich Nhat Hahn, the great Buddhist monk and writer, says that "The most important thing is to find peace and then share it with others."

So, that's our job here: To locate that peace within ourselves first.

Once we have that, then we can create peace in the world. We transform the world by transforming ourselves, much like Mychal did when he accepted the Eleventh Step.

It's like the peace song which says, "Let peace begin with me. Let this be the moment *now*. With every step I take, let this be my solemn vow. To take *each moment*, and live *each moment* in peace eternally. Let there be peace on earth, and let it begin with me."

But how do we find that peace when we live in such a chaotic and stressful world? The answer is that we must align our will with God's will. You know how people go to the chiropractor for an adjustment? Well, we need to align our minds with Spirit. Marianne Williamson, author of *Everyday Grace*, among many other books, says, "When our minds are aligned with Spirit, then God's will is accomplished. Outside of that divine alignment, we are vulnerable to the ego, where chaos rules."

So, how do we do practice surrender, practice abandoning ourselves to the Divine will? If we just let go and let God, and keep our hands off the steering wheel, aren't we in essence just doing nothing? Well, not exactly. Surrender is a discipline, and - if we are disciples - we need to practice this discipline.

Wayne Dyer says that surrender "doesn't mean that we don't have a voice in what happens to us - we do, but the voice only becomes activated when we get our ego out of the way and realign with Spirit." So, how do we put this discipline into practice? Well, first and foremost, is meditation. We must "be still and know" each day, to synch our breath with the Divine breath, so we become one breath. Marianne Williamson says, "When you learn to be really still, you are surrendering your mind to God."

Though that half hour or so of solitude in the morning is crucial, we also need to practice this connection throughout our day, like Brother Lawrence and Mychal did with the Jesus Prayer.

Find the prayer or mantra or word that works bests for you. Surround yourself with positive words that call you back to the presence of Spirit. Maybe simply say "peace" to yourself throughout the day, especially when you're feeling stressed. The Hindu mantra, "shanti, shanti, shanti" is "peace, peace, peace."

When we're feeling good, we're feeling God. That's how we know when we're in alignment with Spirit. If we're not feeling good, that's our signal to surrender.

It's our job to change our thinking so that it's vibrating to a frequency that matches God's energy. That's what the alignment is all about. In doing so, we become a channel for Spirit. Life happens not TO us but THRU us.

Deepak Chopra says that almost all creative works happen in this state when the tenet "thy will be done" is put into practice. He calls this "effortless creation," which involves letting go of the outcome.

The first of The Beatitudes reads, "Blessed are the poor in Spirit/The Kingdom of Heaven is theirs." Being poor in Spirit means being so reliant on God's will for everything, and when we have that, we have the kingdom of heaven, which is this state of peacefulness.

Father Bede Griffiths, a Benedictine monk who started an ashram in India, blending Christian and Hindu spiritualities, wrote beautifully of surrender in his autobiography, *The Golden String*.

He writes, "To discern the divine will and to adhere to it with one's own will is the goal of life. The only proper use of our freedom is freely to will what the divine providence wills for us, to conform our wills by a free act of choice to the divine will.

This is what it means by 'He who will lose his life for my sake will find it.' I have finally realized that the will of God was not to be found in following my own plans, however spiritual they might seem, but in seeking to adapt myself to those circumstances in which by divine providence I actually found myself in. To identify oneself with the will of God is, indeed, the source of all happiness, the source of all peace."

THE WORD:

Here I am, Lord. It is I Lord.
I have heard you calling in the night.
I will go, Lord, where you lead me.
I will hold your people in my heart.
- Isaiah 6:8

"Abandon all varieties of religion and fully
surrender to Me alone. I shall grant you
freedom from all misfortune - do not despair!"
-Bhagavad-Gita (verse 18:66)

CLOSING PRAYER:

"I abandon myself into your hands; do with
me what you will. Whatever you may do, I
thank you. I am ready. I accept all."
- Charles de Foucauld

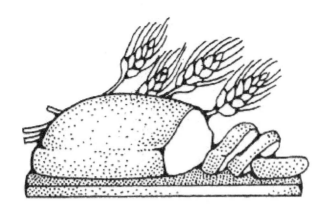

CHAPTER TWO

LET ME MEET WHO YOU WANT ME TO MEET

THEME: Oneness

OPENING PRAYER:

I know that every person - regardless of nationality, faith, lifestyle or tradition - originates from the same Divine Source. Just like spokes on a wheel, we all connect at the Center and move in unison, so no one is ever truly a stranger. In every face, I see my own face, I see the face of God.

ABOUT MYCHAL:

Mychal's daily interactions put him in contact with all types of people, "from beggars to billionaires," as I once commented to him.

At the time of our working together, Mychal would often start his day out at the breadline ministering to the homeless people right outside his door, and, later, he'd often be seen embracing "his regulars": elderly women parishioners who attended daily Mass.

Depending on his schedule, Mychal might spend the day ministering to people with AIDS at Bellevue, where most of the patients were poor, or he might be at NYU Medical Center, a much more upscale facility.

At the former, Mychal would often be dealing with drug addicts living in tenements, and at the latter, he might be having lunch down in the hospital cafeteria with an affluent parent whose college-educated son was in an upstairs room dying of the disease.

One summer night, on our way to an AIDS benefit in Manhattan, Mychal and I were approached by two homeless men asking for money. Rather than simply handing them a few dollars and then continuing on our way, Mychal suggested treating the men to a meal at the Burger King across the street.

As the four of us walked across the busy New York City street - Mychal and I in our religious habits and the two men in tattered clothing - Mychal engaged the men in friendly banter, remarking, "Such a beautiful night, isn't it?"

Once seated inside the restaurant with their burgers in front of them, the men said grace following Mychal's lead. Before taking our leave, Mychal hugged the men, gave them each a blessing, and told them that God loved them.

A twenty-minute walk later, Mychal and I found ourselves in a completely different environment. We were now in the gold-ceiling ballroom of a swanky midtown hotel for an AIDS benefit, surrounded by wealthy New York society types and celebrities like Phil Donahue and Marlo Thomas.

One of the celebrities who approached Mychal that night was actor Christopher Reeve. This was a few years before the horseback riding accident which left him a quadriplegic. I was completely star struck, but Mychal greeted the actor as if they were lifelong friends.

"Such a beautiful night," Mychal remarked, and, later, during and after the meal, there was grace and thanks and hugs. As I watched him in action, I came to the realization that Mychal was no different here than he was with the homeless men. Regardless of class or race, Mychal looked at each person with deep interest and concern, holding their gaze and being completely present.

Mychal's ministry to all people remained just as firm, if not more so, in the years to follow. No one was a stranger, because Mychal recognized the Oneness which binds all people together.

Whether sitting on a cot talking to a destitute man in a homeless shelter, shooting the breeze with a bunch of macho firefighters at a New York City firehouse, or laughing raucously with a group of gay men following a Dignity mass, Mychal had the amazing ability to socialize and empathize with everyone to whom he came in contact.

COMMENTARY:

It's been said that we are all angels who only have one wing, so we need each other to fly.

Imagine waking up each morning exclaiming with wonder, "I can't wait to discover the 'angel' I will meet this day!" or "I can't wait to see how God will use me this day to be an 'angel' to someone today!"

Watch how you'll go about your day not full of dread, but full of joy and excitement, looking for the Christ-light in all you encounter.

We often go about our day absentmindedly, not really paying attention to the clerk at the grocery store or the gas station attendant. We may greet a co-worker with a "How ya doin'?" as we pass in a hallway, but we're not really expecting an intimate conversation.

What if the people you encountered each day were actually here to give you an opportunity to serve? Maybe he or she is there to help you to practice patience or provide an outlet for you to become more selfless?

I recently read a magazine story about a woman and her husband who had to travel out of state for his surgery at a top-notch medical facility. Not knowing anyone in the city, the two checked into their hotel and sat in the room all afternoon with their minds on the next day's surgery.

The husband suggested that they go down to the lobby and do some shopping to take their minds off the surgery. Trying on clothes at a women's clothing boutique, the wife started chatting with the salesclerk, informing her of her husband's upcoming surgery and the week-long recovery period in the hospital.

A few days later, the wife, tired, hungry and disheveled, was sitting next to her husband's hospital bed when in walked the salesclerk. The clerk said to the woman, "I'm here to relieve you. Go back to the hotel, nap, shower, get something to eat. I'll take good care of him while you're gone."

Imagine what the world would be like if more of us were like this salesclerk coming to the assistance of a stranger. That's what we are called to do.

As Jesus taught, "Whatever you do for one of the least of your brothers and sisters of mine, you do for me. For I was hungry and you gave me something to eat. I was thirsty and you gave me something to drink. I was a stranger and you invited me in. I needed clothes and you clothed me. I was sick and you looked after me. I was in prison and you came to visit me."

We can learn a lot from watching the geese flying in "V" formation. It is a fact that lifting power of many wings can achieve twice the distance of any bird flying solo and that their honking sound is meant to encourage one another to keep going.

Additionally, should a bird in formation become ill and fall to the ground, two other birds in the formation will fly down and stay with it until it recovers or dies. Then, they will rejoin another formation.

How do we encourage our fellow brothers and sisters as they journey with us on this road of life? Are we there to help them heal when they fall? Reflect on the people who have encouraged and supported you during times when you were too weak to continue your flight.

Being an angel and helping someone else to fly does not have to involve feeding, clothing, visiting, etc. Our state of peacefulness creates a vibration which greatly impacts our world. This is why meditation is so important. In that still, small place of silence, our prayers of wholeness for others and peace for our world are some of the greatest ways we can be of service.

"Find peace within and be a giver of love and peace to others...Christ saw the Divine in everyone...He looked beyond their human flaws to their true self...We, too, can practice the loving, non-judgmental attitude that comes in realizing, 'My God is in that soul,'" wrote Sri Daya Mata of the Self Realization Fellowship.

When we align ourselves with Spirit's will, the people we encounter each day are Divinely guided to us and we to them. Sometimes, something as simple as a smile or a kind word may be just what someone needs to be lifted up, and when we lift others up, we, too, are lifted.

THE WORD:

"Christ has no body but yours,
No hands, no feet on earth but yours,
Yours are the eyes with which he looks
Compassion on this world,
Yours are the feet with which he walks to do
good,
Yours are the hands, with which he blesses all
the world.
Yours are the hands, yours are the feet,
Yours are the eyes, you are his body.
Christ has no body now but yours,
No hands, no feet on earth but yours,
Yours are the eyes with which he looks
compassion on this world.
Christ has no body now on earth but yours."
-Teresa of Avila

"God is the Father, Earth the Mother. With all things and in all things, we are relative."
- Native American (Sioux)

"Full of love for all things in the world, practicing virtue in order to benefit others, this man alone is happy."
- Buddhism

"See to be in harmony with all your neighbors; love in amity with your brethren."
- Confucianism

"No one is a believer until he loves for his neighbor, and for his brother, what he loves for himself."
- Islam

"Thou shalt love thy neighbor as thyself."
- Judaism

"Do not forget that the world is one great family...Regard heaven as your father, Earth as your Mother, and all things as your brothers and sisters."
- Shintoism

"A man abstains a proper rule of action by looking on his neighbor as himself."
- Hinduism

"A new commandment I give you: That you love one another...By this all men will know that you are my disciples, if you have love for one another." - Christianity

CLOSING PRAYER:

"Continue to love each other like brothers, and remember always to welcome strangers, for by doing this, some people have entertained angels without knowing it."

- Hebrews 13:1-2

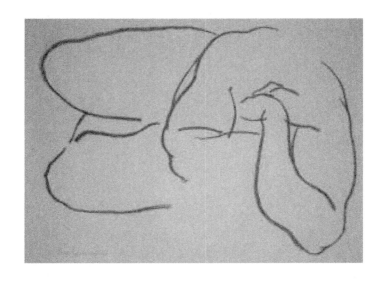

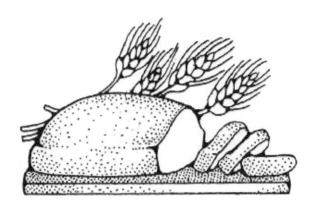

CHAPTER THREE:

TELL ME WHAT YOU WANT ME TO SAY

THEME: Wisdom

OPENING PRAYER:

From Unity, *Let Go and Let God*:

"I want to serve God, to surrender my need to control and be open to the love and will of God. It is through an open mind and heart that love, light and life become fully expressed in me and my life.

Here and now, I commit to let go and let God. I speak the words, "Here I am!" to affirm my openness to God's guidance.

Here and now, I dedicate myself to becoming more attuned to the wisdom of God, knowing I am being guided to my good."

ABOUT MYCHAL:

Mychal formed Saint Francis AIDS Ministry not only to minister to people with AIDS, but also to minister to their family members, caregivers and friends, as well.

To that effect, Mychal suggested a monthly support group called "AIDS and the Gospel." This would be an evening where all affected by the disease could gather together in support and prayer.

I thought it was an excellent idea, until Mychal called me and another young brother, Fran, to his room one afternoon. Looking at us with those bright eyes of his, Mychal said, "I will not be able to attend the first support group, so I'm putting the night in your hands."

Fran and I were both in our early twenties, and neither one of us had any experience in leading a support group. The AIDS crisis was at its peak in New York City at that time, and there was still a lot of fear and panic. Why would Mychal ask two young novices to take the leadership position on such an important task?

It wasn't like he was even asking us, rather was simply stating it as truth. I looked over at Fran, and he seemed as incredulous as I, yet he said, "Okay."

I may have slightly nodded my head somewhat, but that was the extent of my consent. Inside, I was desperately trying to think of ways to get myself out of this tremendous responsibility.

The next day, I approached Mychal and said, "I don't think I can do this. People who have had years of training in counseling would have a difficult time doing this. What if somebody freaks out? What would I do?"

"This is not about you," Mychal firmly but gently admonished, reminding me of his words when we first started the ministry: "We are God's agents on Earth."

The word "agent" stayed on my mind that day. I knew that an agent (like a talent agent or a literary agent) was "someone representing someone else; someone who speaks on another's behalf." So, Mychal was right: Our role was to be God's spokespeople, if you will.

If what I was going to be doing with the support group was truly an act of service and not of ego, then I, like the call of Jeremiah (see this chapter's "The Word" section), would not need to worry about what to say. I would be protected and provided with all I needed for the task at hand.

As Fran and I gathered the twenty or so participants in a circle on the night of our first prayer support group meeting, I was surprisingly calm, knowing that I was there to accomplish God's will, not mine. We dimmed the lights and lit a candle in the center of the circle.

After leading the group in some formal prayers, Fran and I simply let go and let the participants speak their worries, their fears, their anger, and, surprisingly, their blessings. Afterwards, as we turned the lights back on, I noticed Mychal standing in the doorway. He was there all along, smiling like a proud father.

On another occasion, Mychal asked if I would accompany him to a Catholic grammar school in Queens, New York to collect gifts the students had made for people with AIDS. A few weeks earlier, Mychal told us that he had written all the Catholic grammar schools in New York City asking administrators if their students would be interested in helping our AIDS ministry by collecting toiletries.

Of all the schools in the city, the first to respond just happened to be my old grammar school, Saint Helen's in Howard Beach. Now that I think about it, this was a very radical thing for Catholic school children to be doing in 1988, especially since most of the people with AIDS at the time were gay men and IV drug users.

As we walked through the corridors of my old school, greeting many of my former elementary school teachers, Mychal and I stopped into each and every classroom to collect the gift-wrapped shoeboxes that students had filled with shaving cream, razors, deodorant, toothbrushes, and toothpaste.

After we thanked them, the children then had time to ask us questions about our ministry. It was amazing to watch Mychal talk about AIDS with children at each grade level, answering each of their questions with age-appropriate and loving responses. The most often asked question from students was if we were ever afraid. "Never be afraid to love," Mychal responded.

In one eighth-grade classroom, however, one boy asked, "How can you help gay people and drug users?" I looked over at Mychal, but he was giving the floor to me. I responded, "Jesus said, 'Whatever you do for the least of my brothers, you do for me.' And, right now in our society, who's the least?"

At the time, I wasn't quite sure where those words came from, but I know now. In retrospect, I've come to see that with the prayer group and in the classroom, Mychal was giving me the opportunity to open myself up to and trust in Divine guidance and wisdom. He could have stepped in, but I think he wanted me to experience firsthand what he meant by "Tell me what you want me to say."

COMMENTARY:

When someone in our lives is faced with a serious illness, a family tragedy or the death of a loved one, it can often be awkward to know what to say. We want to be of comfort, but we fear being trite or saying the wrong thing.

Our fear can get in the way of our being present for others in their times of need. How comforting to know that when we align ourselves with Spirit, we become a channel and the Divine works through us, giving us just the right words to speak.

John's gospel begins, "In the beginning was the Word: the Word was with God and the Word was God." The Word was made flesh in Jesus and in you and me, so we have the Divine words in us, if only we would get out of the way of our human egos and fears which keep those words at bay.

Of course, it is important to think before we speak, yet sometimes in our nervousness, we speak too quickly in our attempt to fill the void of silence. A wonderful affirmation comes to us from the Book of Psalms: "May the words of my mouth and the meditation of my heart be pleasing to You."

As Father Mychal Judge reminds us, when we ask in love and not in fear, "Lord, tell me what you want me to say," and we do not receive any words, then it's our role to be silent. Sometimes, words get in the way when all that's needed is a shoulder to cry on in a situation that simply just requires our presence.

The Tao Te Ching states, "Those who know do not talk. Those who talk do not know." This, the writer Lao-Tzu says, is "the highest state of man." So, though God is the Word, we do not really have the words to explain God or need words to communicate God's love to others.

Our eyes are called windows to the soul. Sometimes, all that's needed is to look, really look and make eye contact with another. When we do so, we are giving them our full attention, letting them know that we see, value and acknowledge them.

If the words of Divine Mind do come, don't allow your human mind to block their flow with worries of how they will be perceived by others. Silence your ego, which is concerned with appearance, and just allow the Divine to speak through you.

The Word often speaks to us during the silence of our meditations, guiding us to just the right words to use and the actions to take. If you're ever unsure how to proceed in a certain situation, bring your questions and concerns to this sacred moment of prayer and communion with God. Be still and know.

The disciples of Jesus who were gathered in the upper room on Pentecost began speaking in tongues. They spoke "as the Spirit gave them utterance." Though their mouths were moving, the words they were speaking were not their own, but Divinely inspired.

I've heard several spiritual writers and ministers today say a similar thing often happens to them when they are composing or giving a message to their congregations. I myself have sometimes had that experience when writing my books. Often, I look back on what I wrote in awe and say, "I don't even remember writing that!"

If the "upper room" symbolizes our higher consciousness, then when we think, act and live in this state, we will also learn to "speak in tongues," letting the Highest version of ourselves do the talking...or the not talking, if She so chooses.

However, we must keep in mind the words from Corinthians: "If I speak in the tongues of men and of angels, but have not love, I am only a resounding gong or a clanging cymbal." When you come from a place of love, you will never have to fear saying the wrong thing. Your love is louder than words.

THE WORD:

The word of Yahweh was addressed to me, saying:

*'Before I formed you in the womb I knew you;
before you came to birth I consecrated you;
I have appointed you as prophet to the
nations'.*

I said, *'Ah, Lord Yahweh; look, I do not
know how to speak: I am a child!"*

But Yahweh replied:
*'Do not say, "I am a child."
Go now to those to whom I send you
and say whatever I command you.
Do not be afraid of them,
for I am with you to protect you -
it is Yahweh who speaks!"*

Then Yahweh put out his hand and
touched my mouth and said to me:

'There! I am putting my words into your mouth.
Look, today I am sending you
over nations and over kingdoms,
to tear up and to knock down,
to destroy and to overthrow,
to build and to plant.'

-Jeremiah 1: 4-11

CLOSING PRAYER:

"Take all my freedom, my liberty, my will.
All that I have you've given to me,
So I offer it up to you.
I surrender it all to Jesus.
I surrender it all to your will.
I surrender it all for the kingdom of God.
I surrender my life, my all.
Your grace and your love are wealth enough for me.
Grant me these, Lord Jesus Christ,
And I ask for nothing more."

-St. Ignatius of Loyola

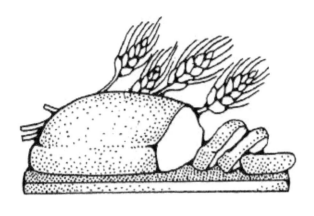

CHAPTER FOUR:

KEEP ME OUT OF YOUR WAY

THEME: Dissolution of Ego

OPENING PRAYER:

"Past and future veil God from our sight; burn up both of them with fire."
-Rumi

"Time is what keeps the light from reaching us. There is no greater obstacle to God than time."
-Meister Eckhart

ABOUT MYCHAL:

Wherever he was, Father Mychal Judge was usually the center of attention. Part of the reason for this was purely physical. Mychal was tall and handsome and was almost always wearing his Franciscan habit. Even in a city like New York, where anything goes, the sight of a man in a monk's robe and sandals riding the subway was unusual and garnered him stares.

At the time I had entered religious life, the custom of wearing a religious habit had gone by the wayside. Though some nuns, brothers and priests were still walking the streets in their religious garb, most were now wearing secular clothing for most of the day.

I asked Mychal once why he still wore the brown monk's robes. "People see a policeman in uniform and know to go to him for help, right?" he said. "I want people to see me on the street and know they can come to me for spiritual help."

In that regard, I think Mychal liked being seen. Friars who lived and worked with him have commented that he loved to have his picture taken, especially when he first donned his fire chaplain's uniform for a professional photographer. He loved the camera, and the camera loved him.

Mychal's work often brought him the spotlight, as well. Befriending a celebrated police officer paralyzed in the line of duty, comforting relatives of those killed in a major airline disaster, or marching openly with the first gay group allowed in the Saint Patrick's Day parade, Mychal was often front and center.

Not everyone would be comfortable in this position, and maybe that's why Mychal gravitated towards such high profile situations. While others might shy away from newsworthy media events, for Mychal this was one way he could use his gifts to be the public face of God.

The last line of Mychal's prayer ("and keep me out of your way") was most likely his reminder to self to keep his ego in check, to make sure that the attention he was receiving was not for his benefit, but for the bigger picture.

When religious figures such as Mahatma Gandhi, Mother Teresa or the Dali Lama have attended public events, their presence has often helped shine the spotlight on the plight of those who are often ignored by the media and the society at large. I think Mychal's motivations were in the same vein.

It should come as no surprise then that God called Mychal to the World Trade Center on September 11, 2001, for the photograph of Mychal's body being carried from the site remains, for many of us, the most ingrained image in our memories of that day.

Ten years later, the names and faces of the terrorists have faded away for many of us, but Mychal's image remains. His selfless act that day continues to shine the light of God's presence in the face of despair.

COMMENTARY:

Our faithfulness and our service to others are wonderful things, and, sometimes, they can even bring public recognition, as they did for many of the great sainted figures. The question to keep in the forefront is: Am I using public recognition to bring healing or to build up my ego?

I used to think that ego was a term that didn't apply to me. I reserved this word for the self-absorbed beauty queen, the Wall Street mogul, or the blinged out rapper. As I've grown in consciousness, I've come to understand that ego is what Buddhists refer to as the incessant "monkey mind" chatter in our head that keeps our focus away from the Present moment, which is where our Spirit lives. I like how Dr. Wayne Dyer refers to ego as standing for Edging God Out, for it truly does keep us from reconnecting with our Spirit.

You may wonder why I use the term *"reconnecting"* rather than *"connecting."* It's because we come from Spirit. We *are* Spirit, so we can never really be disconnected. It's just that we've forgotten that we are Light.

Think of it as a pilot light. The Light has always been on inside you, but you've forgotten to turn it up, so to speak. The ego wants you to keep your pilot light dim, because once you increase the intensity of the flame, the ego will be burned away.

Controlling those negative thoughts is one of the most difficult tasks, but it's imperative to do so in order to release the true brilliance of your Light Divine. The ego wants to control. Spirit asks us to let go and surrender.

Have you ever heard the story of the "Two Wolves"? It's an old Cherokee story, in which a tribal leader tells his grandson about the battle which goes on inside of all people.

"My son, the battle is between two wolves inside us all," the old Cherokee said. "One represents anger, jealousy, sorrow, envy, regret, arrogance, greed, self-pity, ego, false pride, superiority, anxiety, guilt, and inferiority.

"The other wolf represents peace, joy, serenity, humility, kindness, compassion, empathy, hope, truth, love and generosity."

The grandson thought about this for a few minutes, and then asked his grandfather, "So, which wolf wins the battle?"

The old Cherokee replied, "The one you feed."

Feeding the second wolf instead of the first one takes lots of practice, but please don't let that discourage you from commencing on what you'll find is a life-changing (and a life-giving) exercise.

The key is to stay in the present. Why does staying in the present help you to control your negative thoughts? Well, think about it: most negative thoughts we tell ourselves are either about things that happened in the past or things that may happen in the future.

Since the past is over and the future doesn't yet exist, all you have is the Now moment. Centuries ago, Buddha wrote "The secret of health for both mind and body is not to mourn for the past or worry about the future, but to live in the present moment."

In this now moment, we learn to let go of trying to control the outcome. "Nothing will be done through striving or vainglory," says Scripture, and learning to surrender to the present means being so reliant on God's will for everything. When we have that, we have the kingdom of heaven, which is the state of bliss and peacefulness.

St. John of the Cross beautifully wrote, "I have abandoned all I ever sought to be, and in dying, my Spirit has been released." He, obviously, was not talking about his physical death, but the death of his ego, of his need to direct the outcome of his life. Relying solely on God's guidance (Divine "GPS"), he was able to let go and let God, allowing himself to be carried in the Divine Flow of Life.

THE WORD:

Heaven is eternal - the earth endures.
Why do heaven and earth last forever?
they do not live for themselves only.
This is the secret of their durability.

For this reason the sage puts himself last
and so ends up ahead.
he stays a witness to life,
so he endures.

Serve the needs of others,
and all your own needs will be fulfilled.
Through selfless action, fulfillment is attained.

-TAO TE CHING

CLOSING PRAYER:

"My Lord God,
I have no idea where I am going.
I do not see the road ahead of me.
I cannot know for certain where it will end.
Nor do I really understand myself,
and the fact that I think I am following your
will does not mean that I am actually doing so.
But I believe that the desire to please you
does in fact please you.
And I hope I have that desire in all that I am
doing.
I hope that I will never do anything apart from
that desire.
And I know that if I do this you will lead me
by the
right road, though I may know nothing about
it.
Therefore will I trust you always though I may
seem to be lost and in the shadow of death.
I will not fear, for you are ever with me, and
you will never leave me to face my troubles
alone."

-Thomas Merton

76

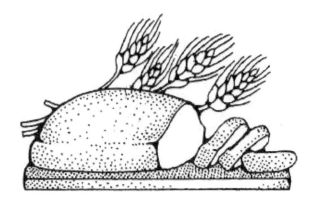

MYCHAL AND THE PEACE PRAYER OF SAINT FRANCIS OF ASSISI

An ordained member of the Franciscan Order of Friars Minor for forty years, Father Mychal Judge certainly had a great devotion to Saint Francis of Assisi. Mychal's attraction to the great saint dates back to childhood.

As a boy, Mychal shined shoes at New York's Penn Station to earn money for his family, as his father died when he was just six years old. Outside the train station, young Mychal would often see the Franciscan friars in their brown habits walking to and from St. Francis of Assisi Church on nearby West 31st Street. Mychal said he knew there and then that he wanted to be a friar.

Mychal moved into the friary on 31st Street in 1986, and he lived there until his death. His third-floor bedroom window looked out at Engine 1/Ladder 23 firehouse, and often he took meals to the firefighters he served there in his role as NYFD chaplain.

In 1988, when people with AIDS were still much feared, Mychal had the idea to create St. Francis AIDS Ministry on the first floor of the friary where he lived. He and the other friars also continued to serve the homeless outside their door by providing hot soup and bread, and the St. Francis Breadline continues to this day.

Father Michael Duffy said, "Francis had a certain natural bent for compassion. I think Mychal Judge did, too. That's what made him such a good Franciscan. He just felt so bad for people who were not cared for."

Thinking back on Mychal's years as a Franciscan, one can't help but notice the parallels between his life of service and the ideals St. Francis of Assisi set forth in his beloved Peace Prayer.

I hope that as you reflect on Francis's beautiful prayer below, you will not only be inspired by Mychal's examples of service, but that you will also consider the ways you can serve as an "instrument of peace" in your own world today:

LORD,

MAKE ME AN INSTRUMENT OF YOUR PEACE.

WHERE THERE IS HATRED, LET ME SOW LOVE.

In 1998, 1999 and 2000, Mychal accompanied his good friend, NYPD detective Stephen McDonald, to Northern Ireland on peace missions of reconciliation between Catholics and Protestants. The two men become close after Stephen had been shot in the line of duty in 1986, leaving him a quadriplegic. In Ireland, Mychal pushed Stephen's wheelchair along cobblestone streets where they, as Catholics, and Mychal in his Franciscan habit, ventured into hostile territory.

Lord, how may I help You turn hated into love?

WHERE THERE IS INJURY, PARDON.

Mychal was a long-standing member of Dignity, a group for gay and lesbian Catholics. In 1986, Cardinal O'Connor banned the group from meeting at any of the diocesan churches in New York City. In response, Mychal welcomed the group into St. Francis of Assisi church, which was under Franciscan and not diocesan control. "Is there so much love in the world that we can afford to discriminate against any kind of love?" Mychal often asked.

Lord, how may I help You fight for justice?

WHERE THERE IS DOUBT, FAITH.

"Does God love me?" Mychal was asked as he visited a man dying of AIDS. Mychal responded by kissing and hugging the man, and rocking him silently in his arms. Many who were suffering from the disease were uneasy with a representative of the church coming to visit them, as many had been told it was their sinful behavior that had brought on God's wrath. Mychal allayed their fears and their doubts, often by simply rubbing their feet and telling them that God loves them.

Lord, how may I bring faith in You to a doubting world?

WHERE THERE IS DESPAIR, HOPE.

The plight of the homeless, especially in a large metropolis like New York City, can be overwhelming, causing many citizens to simply turn a blind eye to the despair felt by their fellow brothers and sisters. Mychal responded: sometimes with money, sometimes with food, sometimes with a warm coat off his back, and always with love.

Lord, how may I bring hope to those in despair?

WHERE THERE IS DARKNESS, LIGHT.

September 11, 2001 remains one of the darkest days in American history. Yet, on that day, amidst all the darkness and destruction, Mychal Judge was a beacon of light, the Light of God's shining love.

Lord, how may I bring Your Light to a world in darkness?

WHERE THERE IS SADNESS, JOY.

In 1996, after the crash of TWA Flight 800 on Long Island, Mychal Judge spent more than two straight weeks ministering to the grieving family members of those who had lost their lives. Mychal comforted their sadness and brought them the message of the joy of eternal life.

Lord, how may I comfort the sorrowful and bring Your joy?

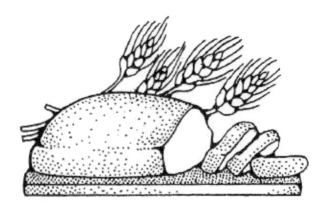

THE LAST HOMILY OF
FATHER MYCHAL JUDGE

Given on September 10, 2001, the day before his
death, at the FDNY's Engine 73, Ladder 42
firehouse in the Bronx, New York:

"Good morning, everyone.

May the grace of God the Father, peace of God the Son, and the fellowship of the Holy Spirit be with you all.

We come to this house this morning to celebrate renewal, rejuvenation, new life. We come to thank God for the blessings over all the years - the good work that's been done here and especially the last few days. We can never thank God enough for the reality of the lives we have. So, standing in His presence this morning, and truly this is a chapel, let us pause for a moment, perhaps close our eyes, and thank God for some special blessings in our individual lives.

Let us pray.

Thank you Lord for life. Thank you for love. Thank you for goodness. Thank you for work. Thank you for family. Thank you for friends. Thank you for every gift because we know that every gift comes from you, and without you, we have and are nothing. So, as we celebrate this day in thanksgiving to you, keep our hearts and minds open.

Let us enjoy each other's company, and most of all, let us be conscious of Your presence in our lives and in a special way in the lives of all those who have gone before us. And Father we make our prayer, as always, in Jesus' name who lives with You forever and ever.

That's the way it is. Good days. And bad days. Up days. Down days. Sad days. Happy days. But never a boring day on this job. You do what God has called you to do. You show up. You put one foot in front of another. You get on the rig and you go out and you do the job - which is a mystery. And a surprise. You have no idea when you get on that rig. No matter how big the call. No matter how small. You have no idea what God is calling you to. But he needs you. He needs me. He needs all of us.

The retirees - He needs your prayers. He needs your stopping by occasionally to give strength and support and to tell the stories of the old days. We need the house and to those of you that are working now, keep going. Keep supporting each other. Be kind to each other. Love each other. Work together and do what you did the other night and the weeks and the months and the years before and from this house, God's blessings go forth in this community. It's fantastic!

What great people. We love the job. We all do. What a blessing that is. A difficult, difficult job and God calls you to it. And then He gives you a love for it so that a difficult job will be well done. Isn't He a wonderful God? Isn't He good to you? To each one of you? And to me! Turn to Him each day. Put your faith and your trust and your hope and your life in His hands, and He'll take care of you and you'll have a good life.

And this house will be a great, great blessing to this neighborhood and to this city.

Amen."

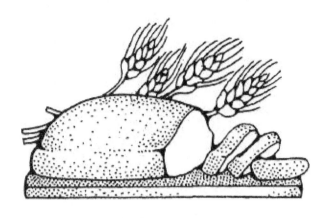

SERENITY PRAYER

A long-standing member of Alcoholics Anonymous, Father Mychal Judge surely found great strength and comfort in the organization's Serenity Prayer. In fact, Mychal had a framed needle-point rendering of the prayer on a wall in his room.

In praying for the serenity to accept what he could not change (say, his homosexuality or the Catholic hierarchy), the courage to change what he could change (his drinking or ego), and the wisdom to know the difference, Mychal was able to be a more authentic and joyous reflection of God's image.

Whether or not you are suffering from alcoholism, the Serenity Prayer is another wonderful way of praying for peace within yourself. As Thomas a Kempis, the medieval monk, wrote, "First keep peace within yourself, then you can also bring peace to others."

This is what Mychal did, and it's your call, too.

**God grant me the serenity
to accept the things I cannot change;
courage to change the things I can;
and wisdom to know the difference.
Living one day at a time;
Enjoying one moment at a time;
Accepting hardships as the pathway to
peace;
Taking, as He did, this sinful world
as it is, not as I would have it;
Trusting that He will make all things right
if I surrender to His Will;
That I may be reasonably happy in this life
and supremely happy with Him
Forever in the next.
Amen.**

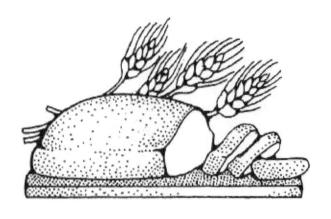

MYCHAL: MAN OF THE BEATITUDES

"The Kingdom of Heaven" that Jesus describes in his Sermon on the Mount is not some future place in the sky or anywhere outside of us. It is within us and it is here and now.

The Beatitudes are Jesus instructions for us - his direction map, if you will - for attaining this state of being.   Whether or not Mychal Judge was consciously using the Beatitudes as the blueprint for his life, the following translation from the original Aramaic (the language Jesus spoke) demonstrates that Mychal was truly a man of the Beatitudes.

As you pray with these beautiful words given to us by one who had attained this highest state of consciousness, contemplate the ways Father Mychal Judge lived these tenets in his own life. Then, set your mind and heart on living out these Truths in your own life:

A heavenly attitude is theirs, those whose home is in Truth; theirs is a heavenly state.

A heavenly attitude is theirs, those mourning their wrongs; they shall be comforted.

A heavenly attitude is theirs, those with humility; they will gain the earth.

A heavenly attitude is theirs, those who hunger and thirst for justness; they shall attain it.

A heavenly attitude is theirs, those whose love is without conditions; they will therefore receive unconditional love.

A heavenly attitude is theirs, those without fault in their minds; they will see God.

A heavenly attitude is theirs, those serving the peace of God; they will be called the children of God.

A heavenly attitude is theirs, those being scorned because of their justness; theirs is the Kingdom of Heaven.

A heavenly attitude is yours when they harass you and scorn you and deceitfully speak against you every evil word because of being with me.

Rejoice, be happy, be joyful at the increase of your reward in achieving heaven for yourself and others.

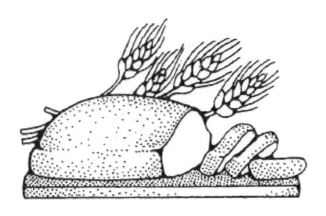

CONCLUSION

The depiction of a loaf of bread was chosen as the header for each section of this book, as I think it serves as a perfect image for Father Mychal Judge's life and message.

During the time of our work together at Saint Francis AIDS Ministry, Mychal took our group of young monks to the Jersey Shore for a weekend retreat. A wealthy parishioner of his had offered us the use of her beautiful beach house for our time together.

Each morning of the retreat, we sat on the floor around the coffee table as Mychal said Mass for us. When it came time for communion, he broke a loaf of bread and passed it around.

"The word 'companion' means 'with bread,'" he told us one morning, reminding us that - as companions - we were here to nourish one another. I have never forgotten that.

"You have no idea what God is calling you to, but he needs you," Mychal implored in his last homily. When I reflect on that, I keep hearing, "God kneads you," and I think about Mychal being living bread for the world.

Permitting himself to be shaped by unseen hands and allowing the yeast of the Spirit to rise up in him, Mychal - like the manna from heaven - provided nourishment to those around him, feeding their bodies, minds and souls.

We, too, are called to be bread for the world, but, like Mychal, we must willingly and lovingly give ourselves over to be shaped and molded, to allow Spirit to lift us, so we can truly provide lasting sustenance for the world.

It is our sole purpose. It is our soul purpose.

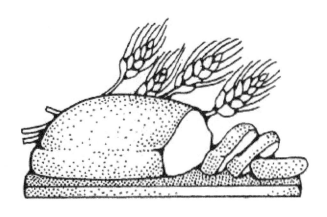

WHO BETTER THAN YOU?

The following essay of mine originally appeared in the anthology *Queer and Catholic* (Routledge Press 2008) and is reprinted with permission:

Walking to the subway station after an AA meeting in Manhattan, Father Mychal Judge, a Franciscan priest fully attired in his hooded brown monk's habit, turned to a young gay man he met at the meeting and said, "Isn't God wonderful!" When the young man asked the priest why, Father Mychal responded, "Look at all the beautiful men out on a Friday night."

What may sound like the introduction to another sordid story about the secret sexual lives of Catholic priests is anything but, for this is the tale of a man who took his vow of celibacy very seriously, yet still celebrated his sexuality openly. A man of God, but still just a man.

Although most would come to know him following his death on September 11, 2001, Father Mychal Judge entered my life in late nineteen eighties, a time when the Catholic Church was beginning its regression back to its pre-Vatican II era of fear and repression. Up until then, my life as a gay Catholic was exceedingly smooth-going.

I was extremely lucky (Mychal would later tell me I was fated) to come of age during a very short window of time in the Catholic Church where 'God Don't Make Junk' was becoming the company's new motto. The young nuns, priests and brothers who taught me were products of the "peace and love"-era movement of the nineteen sixties. They wore bell-bottoms and Birkenstocks under their habits and sang joyful Kumbaya-like folk-songs about loving one another. The catechism taught for decades was replaced with "The Good News." This contrasted sharply with the pre-Vatican II era church of my parents' generation, where priests said mass in Latin with their backs to the congregation and morose hymns were sung about fearing the Lord's wrath.

On the walls of my Catholic elementary school, for example, all the spooky looking pictures of Jesus with the sacred heart bursting out of his chest were replaced with newer portraits of a more approachable, smiling, handsome Jesus. This figure was not some untouchable icon to be feared. Rather, I remember praying to this image and finding comfort. As a sensitive artistic kid growing up in a very Italian working-class Queens neighborhood, I often found solace picturing myself being held in the arms of this gentle man whom I was told loved me unconditionally.

It was also at grade school where a very cool young nun - who wore lipstick! - named Sister Eileen first noticed my interest in other boys. While the rest of the sixth-grade boys showed their athletic prowess during gym class, I hid behind the bleachers drawing them - okay, mostly one of them: my crush, Pauly Noto - in my sketchbook. Finding me there one day, Sister Eileen reached down and took the book from my hands. I feared she might reprimand me or, worse yet, force me to join the other boys at play. Flipping through the drawings, however, she smiled and said admiringly, "You have a good eye for the male form." And then, handing the book back to me, said, "That's a gift. Don't hide your light under a bushel basket."

A few years later, at the all boys Catholic high school I attended, Brother Thomas, my history teacher, asked for my help in creating a display for the bulletin board case outside the main office in commemoration of the school's twenty-fifth anniversary. As we worked after school every day for a week on the project, I came to know him as a person, rather than simply an authority figure in religious garb. He later became the first person to whom I confided I was gay. He didn't tell me it was just a phase all boys went through, nor did he tell me I was going to hell. Rather, he gave me a copy of John Reid's book, *The Best Little Boy in the World*, which he inscribed, 'You are God's perfect creation.'

I hear horror stories from strangers, colleagues and friends - both gay and straight - about their growing up Catholic. Stories of ruler-wielding nuns and predatory priests. Guilt, oppression and shame are the keywords they use in describing their experiences in the church. I have no such tales to tell, and maybe that's why as a gay man, I find myself apologizing for having come through my twelve years of Catholic schooling not just unscathed, but uplifted and inspired, while most of my gay brethren were not as fortunate.

I never really struggled thinking that being gay was wrong or sinful, as I had been raised in a church which taught me that I was perfect just how God made me.

It was because of people like Sister Eileen and Brother Thomas that I decided to enter religious life myself after graduating from college and living life as an openly gay man in Manhattan in the nineteen eighties. Like their calling in the sixties, I, too, decided to live counter-culturally in response to the changing climate of the times. The 'greed is good'-yuppie movement and the sexual promiscuity of the gay club scene clashed with the ideals I had for myself and for my generation, and I hoped my commitment to poverty, chastity and obedience would serve as an inspiration.

During my years of religious training in the novitiate, we were encouraged to read *Fully Alive, Fully Human*, a book written by the Jesuit priest, John Powell. In it, he wrote, "We are not prisoners of the past, but pioneers of an exciting future." Unlike the previous generation of clergy whom suffered through and repressed their sexuality for the sake of the Kingdom, we novices learned that we could be sexual and celibate.

We were reminded time and time again that Jesus - although fully God - was also fully a man with all human desires intact. Although we were to lead a chaste life, we were warned not to become asexual beings. And, indeed, I was welcomed into religious life in the Catholic Church as an out gay man by my superiors and religious community.

Which brings me back to Father Mychal Judge and his admiration of all the beautiful men walking the streets of Manhattan that Friday night. His declaration was a joyful expression of his God given gift of sexuality. This was a celebration of a celibate life lived happily and to the full.

Ironically, it was the burgeoning AIDS crisis - a time of great death - that brought me together with this man so full of life. The Catholic Church that I had been brought up in, which had shown me so much acceptance - the very church to which I just committed my life - was beginning to revert back to its former judgmental self. It coincided with the commencement of AIDS and it seemed to happen overnight, though, in retrospect, it had been on a slow boil for quite awhile.

At a time when the church should have come roaring into action - for this is where Jesus would surely have been with the outcasts and the sick - church leaders, instead, chose judgment over love. This was especially true in New York City, one of the places hardest hit with the virus, where Cardinal John O'Connor became the face of hate to the gay community.

While most Catholic clergy members kept their distance, Father Mychal took it upon himself to address the needs of the gay community at this time of crisis. He formed Saint Francis AIDS Ministry, one of the first Catholic AIDS organizations in the country. He, I and three other professed religious men, began to minister to people with AIDS in area hospitals, where we were often met with distrust and, sometimes, hostility from those we visited.

Their reactions were understandable, for the Church had become the enemy. Among many other offenses to gay community, Cardinal O'Connor had banned the gay Catholic group, Dignity - of which Mychal was a member - from meeting in any of his diocese's parishes, and he also supported efforts to keep gays from marching in the Saint Patrick's Day Parade.

Hearing the criticisms of the Church from those to whom I ministered, I began to question my calling, and I found myself becoming anxious each time I entered a patient's hospital room for the first time.   Although a member of the gay community, I was also a representative of the Catholic Church. I had one foot in each camp, and both sides seemed to question where lay my true allegiance.   Even I was becoming unsure. I told Mychal that I felt like I was leading only half a life, to which he responded, quoting from Scripture, "I came that you might have life, and have it to the full."

I knew I couldn't be all things to all people, but Mychal Judge somehow could. Whether sitting on a cot talking to a destitute man in a homeless shelter, shooting the breeze with a bunch of macho firefighters at a New York City firehouse, or schmoozing with some rich society matrons at a swanky benefit, Mychal had the amazing ability to socialize and empathize with everyone to whom he came in contact.

One of these wealthy parishioners volunteered the use of her beach house on the Jersey shore for a week's retreat for our AIDS ministry, so the five of us could get away, renew ourselves, and reflect on the work we were doing.

Knowing my frustrations about the ministry and my doubts about my vocation, Father Judge took me on a long walk along the beach one day that week. After walking in silence for quite awhile just listening to the waves crashing onto the shore, Mychal put his arm around my shoulder and said, "Who better than you?"

"What do you mean?" I asked.

"Let's pretend you're God, okay?" he explained. "You've got these two groups at war with one another, so you need to hire a peacemaker that understands both sides, right? Well, who better than you?"

And then he grabbed both my hands in his and prayed aloud the prayer of Saint Francis, the namesake of our AIDS Ministry: "Lord, make us a means of your peace. Where there is hatred, let us sow love. Where there is injury, pardon. Where's there's darkness, light."

When we arrived back at the beach house, we heard on the evening news that the billionaire Malcolm Forbes had died. The news report recounted the lavish parties, collections of fine art and motorcycle rides with Elizabeth Taylor. "Talk about a full life, huh?" I said.

Mychal didn't say a thing, but his silence spoke volumes.

A few weeks later, the gay writer and activist, Michaelangelo Signorile, would break the news of Forbes's secret gay life on the cover of 'Outweek' magazine, bringing the topic of 'outing' into the mainstream.

There was no such outing, however, following Mychal's death a decade later, for there was nothing to out. He proved that someone openly gay could lead a full, healthy and rewarding life in the Catholic Church. Not a prisoner of the past, Mychal was, indeed, a pioneer of the future.

My own calling, however, was short-lived. I found it increasingly difficult to belong to a church that was becoming more and more exclusive, a church that had even begun to deny gay men from entering the priesthood. The Church was asking me to hide my light under a bushel basket, but I was God's perfect creation, remember?

The poster for 'The Saint of 9/11,' the documentary about Father Judge's life and death, depicts Mychal in his Franciscan robes walking alone along a beach. Staring at that image, I remember our own walk along the beach that day, and I take comfort imaging myself in the arms of this gentle man who loved me unconditionally and who died so I might have life to the full.

Who better than me? I know of one man, for sure.

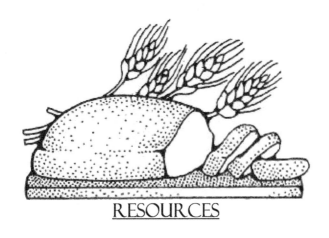

RESOURCES

TO LEARN MORE ABOUT FATHER MYCHAL:

BOOKS:

FATHER MYCHAL JUDGE: AN AUTHENTIC AMERICAN HERO, BY MICHAEL FORD (2002) PAULIST PRESS

THE BOOK OF MYCHAL: THE SURPRISING LIFE AND HEROIC DEATH OF FATHER MYCHAL JUDGE, BY MICHAEL DALY (2008) THOMAS DUNNE BOOKS

HE SAID YES: THE STORY OF FATHER MYCHAL JUDGE, BY KELLY ANN LYNCH (AUTHOR) & M. SCOTT OATMAN (ILLUSTRATOR) (2007) PAULIST PRESS

DVDS:

THE SAINT OF 9/11: THE TRUE STORY OF FATHER MYCHAL JUDGE (2006) NARRATED BY SIR IAN MC KELLAN, ARTS ALLIANCE AMERICA FILMS

THE LAST HOMILY OF FATHER MYCHAL JUDGE (2010) AVAILABLE AT WWW.MYCHALSMESSAGE.ORG

ABOUT THE AUTHOR

Salvatore Sapienza is a former religious brother in the Catholic Church, now pursuing studies as an Interfaith minister. A freelance writer, he has written feature stories for several newspapers and magazines across the country. Sapienza is also the author of the books, *Gay is a Gift* and *Seventy Times Seven*, which was nominated for two Lambda Literary Awards, including Best Spirituality. He and his partner of eighteen years live in Saugatuck, Michigan. Visit www.mychalsprayer.com for more information.

ABOUT THE ILLUSTRATOR

Donna Leonard studied art history at the University of Wisconsin, and then studied line drawing with Sanae' Hagino in Chicago. She received the Kendall Dean's Scholarship for Excellence at Kendall College of Art and Design in Grand Rapids. Her work has been shown at You'nique International Gallery, Caledonia Gallery and Saugatuck Artists Collective. Several of her oil paintings of horses were recently auctioned at Universal Studios in Los Angeles. She and her husband, along with their dog, cats and horses, live in Douglas, Michigan. Visit www.donnaleonardart.com for more information.

Printed in Great Britain
by Amazon

79473090R00068